Meet My Mother

Also by Louise Nicholas

The Smear Test
Haven't you had it yet?
The Mammogram
The Red Shoes (In New Poets Three)
WomanSpeak (with Jude Aquilina)
Large
The List of Last Remaining

Louise Nicholas

Meet My Mother

Acknowledgements

Some of the poems in this collection have been previously published, sometimes in slightly altered form. My thanks to the editors and publishers of the following collections: *The List of Last Remaining*, Five Islands Press 2016; *Large*, Garron Press 2013; *WomanSpeak* (co-authored with Jude Aquilina), Wakefield Press 2009 and to the editors of the following literary journals: *Antipodes* (USA), *Cuttlefish*, *Friendly Street 31*, *Gawler Poetry Readers*, *InDaily*, *Poetrix*, *Quadrant*, *Riverland Writers' Guild* anthologies, *tamba*, *Agenda* (UK), *The Best Australian Poems 2014*.

Thanks also to my fellow poets and mentors – too numerous to name – whose work inspires better poetry than I might otherwise write, and to the slave drivers amongst them – especially Helen Parsons, Jennifer Liston, Janet Thomas and Owen Gallagher – who have held me to deadlines in the writing of this book; to all those at the Strand Café and Restaurant in Glenelg, where much of the writing of this book was done; and to Stephen and Brenda at Ginninderra Press, for their guidance and professionalism.

Meet My Mother
ISBN 978 1 76041 526 6
Copyright © text Louise Nicholas 2018

First published 2018 by
GINNINDERRA PRESS
PO Box 3461 Port Adelaide 5015 Australia
www.ginninderrapress.com.au

Contents

Introduction	9
In Her Own Words: 1	13
The Port Lincoln Years 1945–1966	29
117 degrees in the shade	33
Flashback	34
Picture	35
Chopping the wood	36
23 Tennant Street	37
Making do	38
Skittles	39
The wharfie, the dressmaker and the fifth child	40
Coffin Bay	41
Mum and Uncle Bob	42
In the early evenings then,	43
Tiddalik	44
The Twelve Days of Christmas	45
Return to Adelaide 1966	47
Stroke	51
After the stroke,	52
Card sharp	53
Photograph: Mum on a South Pacific cruise, 1977	54
Triple trounced	56
After falling from a car on the way home from the Teachers' Ball	57
The Letters	59
Reading Mum's letters	62

Her Last Ten Years	83
Photo: Mum with Josh and Zoe	87
Sunday drive	88
A wooden duck, a Christmas tree ornament	89
Family tree	90
General MacArthur makes a call	92
My mother's second husband	93
By the light	94
How to scale a fish	96
I call upon my father	97
'She's gone…'	99
Uninvited	102
Last day	103
On the day of your death,	104
Echolalia	105
Her tennis trophy	106
His moustache	107
Blue dressing gown	108
On becoming my mother	109
In Her Own Words 2	111
Daisy	114
Mum's notebooks	118
Morning	119
Afterword	121
Meet my mother	124
Mum's Recipes	127
List of Photographs	134
Note	134

In memory of
Dorothy Edna Atkinson
(1917–2011)

We are such stuff
As dreams are made on, and our little life
Is rounded with a sleep.

William Shakespeare (*The Tempest*, Act 4 Scene 1)

'I've lived such a little life really.'

Willy Russell (screenwriter, *Shirley Valentine*, 1989)

Introduction

Among the things my mother left behind – her watch, her recipe books, a place in my life that was suddenly, irreversibly, empty – was her dream of being a writer. Year after year, I gave her a notebook and pen. Sometimes she made a start. One year, she completed the twenty-nine handwritten pages of her life story that form the first section of this book. Another year, she completed a YWCA creative writing course.

There were letters too, of course – in the days before emails, when everyone wrote letters – and many of my mother's letters were written in rhyming couplets or quatrains.

But a whole memoir or collection of short stories or poetry? That would have to wait until that 'one day', she said: 'One day when I'm not so busy; one day when I'm not so tired; one day when the time seems right.' But as is the way with so many 'one day's, it never arrived. Or if it did, it was lost when dementia began to worm its way through all she knew and all the words she knew for telling it.

Some people's lives light up the world stage. The vast majority's do not. My mother's life did not. Like Shirley Valentine's, like mine, hers was 'a little life'; a hearthrug-sized life. But little though it was, why not shine a light upon it? Not a bright light perhaps but bright enough and long enough to show that she was here and that she loved life, almost as much as she loved her children, and that she played her part in it for ninety-four years.

This book shines a light on my mother's life. But more than that, by including her words amongst my own, it is an attempt to fulfil her dream, albeit posthumously, of being a published writer.

In Her Own Words: 1

At the insistence of my daughter Louise, and being unable, any longer, to ignore the (subtle!) hints of blank books being among my Christmas gifts, I am at last writing all I know about my life, my parents and the times into which I was born. I have also been influenced by the fact that now I am nearing old age – some would say I'm already there! – I wish, constantly, that I'd listened more intently to my parents' tales of their earlier days. I now have to accept that I really know very little about my mother's background, and tracing back her family tree, which my son John is trying to do, is fraught with difficulties.

My mother was born in Birmingham, England, on 28th November 1889 and was brought up in the town of Walsall. She was the third child of Kate Mary and Samuel Stephen Davies. Their first child, Daisy (who died when she was seven) was followed by Alex, Minnie (my mother) and, several years later, Percy, whom Mother adored. Kate and Samuel were married young and were still only in their mid-twenties by the time their family was complete.

Samuel Stephen, usually called Sam, had been orphaned at birth; his father had died in a railway accident three weeks earlier and his mother, who was French, died in childbirth, so Sam was fostered by a family in Wales (where he was born). Unfortunately, I know nothing of his early life, except that he followed in what one presumes was his father's occupation and eventually became an engineer surveyor. After marrying Kate Warren and having fathered four children, he worked on the Punjab railway in India and only returned to England on furlough every two years. During his absences, Kate's mother moved into the household and took over the cooking and the care of her daughter who, apparently, was not in good health, and seems to have spent a lot of time in bed. For whatever reason, she seems not to have figured very much in my mother's early years. Although she talked constantly of her father and younger brother, she rarely mentioned her mother except to say, 'She was always in bed.'

Meanwhile, with Granny busy in the kitchen (apparently, she was an excellent cook; I did have her cookery book – lost, I fear) and their father in India, Minnie and Percy had an unusual amount of freedom. In an age when girls were taught to cook, sew and perform musically, Minnie became proficient at rifle shooting and could often be seen careering around the neighbourhood on her brother's bicycle, clad in knickerbockers and with her hair pushed up under one of his caps. Needless to say, her father, on leave from India, was horrified to find his beautiful young daughter such a complete tomboy and took steps to correct the situation. He began to take her out socially and instilled in her a love of beautiful clothes, theatre, dancing etc. (Minnie's love of beautiful clothes stayed with her throughout her life and I didn't ever see her untidy or not dressed to perfection.)

It wasn't long before the young men began to be interested and at nineteen she became engaged to a handsome, serious young man, one Jim Clarkson. Under his influence (he sang in the choir), she became an ardent churchgoer and was confirmed in the Anglican faith. However, her father didn't find Jim a suitable husband for his lively, pleasure-loving daughter – thought him far too sober and staid (he was also helping to support his mother) so encouraged her to forgo marriage for a while and travel to Australia with him, where he was interested in discovering what prospects there were for a man with his qualifications. Kate didn't want to leave her mother and England nor, indeed, her two sons, who had not at that time finished their education, but planned to follow her husband and daughter at a later date.

Sam, who at the time of leaving England was still a young man – only in his early forties and tall, blond and good-looking – thoroughly enjoyed the sea voyage and the feminine company available. The ship sailed via South Africa and they disembarked in New Zealand. They stayed there for six months before continuing on to New South Wales, where Minnie was left with her aunt and uncle – Julia and Mark Wilner and their young son Cyril. Julia was Kate's older sister who had migrated to Australia, much against her will, a short time earlier. Although she lived to be ninety-six, she didn't ever feel 'at home' in her new country and always seemed to me to be an unhappy woman. Unfortunately, too, she was widowed when still quite young, and being left with a young son and very little money added to her discontent. To help support Cyril, she gave music lessons and on the rare 'trips' to N.S.W. that we had in my youth, I remember she played the piano beautifully.

Mother found her aunt difficult to live with, and her discipline tiresome and over-strict, especially for a girl who had rarely had any! The only solution seemed to be to find employment and this she did, though she was quite unqualified in every way. Her first employer was a photographer who taught her to retouch and tint photographs, and later she was employed as a companion to an older woman who grew very fond of her and treated her as a member of the family, with plenty of time to herself, enabling her to join a group of young people on outings, picnics etc. It was at one of these outings – an amateur cricket club's picnic – that she met my father, Frank Richard Marshall.

Frank's father, Richard Marshall, and his mother, Elizabeth Hannah Crowle, were married in the Parish Church of St Breward, Bodmin, in the county of Cornwall on 10th January 1880. At that time, they were aged twenty-two and twenty-three respectively. Richard was a farmer and, according to Dad, Elizabeth was a lady's maid. My paternal grandfather could neither read nor write, which was not unusual for a farmer's son; the sons began working on the family farm when quite young and were exempted from attending school. His wife, however, was quite well educated. Even when very old, she wrote excellent letters in a clear hand and was very 'lady-like' in her manner and speech. I only remember her as an elderly lady, usually dressed in black. But she was, in fact, only fifty-nine when I was born, and already had a number of grandchildren.

In the late 1880s, Richard and Elizabeth, with their four young children, migrated to Australia and settled in North Sydney. My father was born in 1890 and several years later, another child, Annie, was born. Dad was only sixteen when his father died as the result of a ruptured appendix. He was forty-nine and left his widow without much in the way of material wealth. For a while, she took in washing, but with Lily becoming a proficient dressmaker and Dad, who was dux of his school, at twenty-one employed at New York Life Insurance Co., life became a little easier. The two older children were already married. The oldest son, Joseph, married a beautiful young girl but when she died during the birth of their second son, Max, Joe promptly left his two young sons with his mother and unmarried sisters, 'borrowed' Dad's best suit and moved to New Zealand. When he notified them several years later that he had remarried, one of his younger sisters took Max over to him. Noel, the older child, stayed with his grandmother until he married at almost middle age. Annie and Lily, the youngest children, remained at home to care for their mother, who was a victim of severe arthritis.

Mother had been welcomed with open arms to the Marshall family, at least by her mother-in-law. (She and my mother maintained a great respect and love for each other; they corresponded regularly until the death of Grandma at ninety-six.) Her sisters-in-law, the unmarried ones, were not quite so affectionate, however – perhaps jealousy had a lot to do with it. They were constant visitors to my parents' first home at North Sydney, and didn't miss an opportunity of criticising mother for her housekeeping, extravagant way of living etc. Mother, of course, couldn't cook and for a while they seem to have lived on baked rabbits. They dined out whenever possible but eventually, with help from a wonderful neighbour, she learnt to cook good plain meals, cared for her house beautifully and became proficient at the art of knitting; sewing, although she tried, was not for her, but I can still remember the beautifully knitted dresses she made for me and my sister.

Shortly after the war, which had claimed the life of Percy, Mother's beloved younger brother, only a few days after Armistice had been signed (the large portrait we had of him showed him to be a tall, good-looking well-built man in his early twenties), Dad was moved to Victoria and became manager of the New York Life Insurance Co. Mother gave birth to my sister, Joyce Eleanor, only a month later. I remember, though I was only two and a half years old, my brother Dick (who was then five) and myself, playing with some older children next door, when Dad came in to get us. He took us down to the garden shed, where there was a large pumpkin with a slice cut from it, and told us we had a baby sister and that she had come in the pumpkin; even then, I wondered how on earth she had managed to get in, the whole thirteen and a half pounds of her!

I wasn't disposed to like the addition to the family much; it amazed me that I was considered big enough to walk everywhere while this great big baby got to be pushed or carried – quite a natural reaction and one which my brother had at the time of my birth; history has it that my grandmother just caught me when Dick grabbed me, at six weeks, by the legs and was about to dump me on the floor, muttering to himself, 'She shan't have MY pram!' Joy continued to grow into a big toddler and I remained a little girl, which is when I was nicknamed Dot.

After moving around into several rented houses, my parents finally bought a house at Camberwell – Stanley Grove, Canterbury – now flats. Dick attended Camberwell Boys' Grammar and in due course I commenced at St Mark's Church of England School. I didn't enjoy it much, mainly because I had to wear boots to strengthen weak ankles (they're still weak!) and was constantly teased. I was also painfully shy and can't remember that I had any best friends. I do remember going to birthday parties, though, so presume there were some. And I did have a playmate nearby, Marjorie Tattnall. She was younger and considered delicate so didn't go to school – at least not then. She was an only child and her mother was always resting and appeared fragile. Their house was very large with a huge garden and they had a live-in maid and a car – all symbols of wealth to my young eyes. Though I loved to go there each day, I constantly had to give in to the spoilt daughter of the house.

When I was seven, New York Life Insurance Co. amalgamated with the National Mutual and Dad was moved to South Australia to become the business manager of NMLA. For some reason, known only to my parents, they decided to auction the house and contents. Joy and I were only allowed to bring a few of our favourite toys; so, presumably, was Dick. The rest were sent to the Children's Hospital, and heaven knows what became of the rocking horse and my beloved dolls' house. Mother obviously thought it time for a completely fresh start.

We moved to South Australia around Christmas time and spent Christmas and a short period afterwards staying with our maternal grandfather at Norwood; he must have just rented the house for a holiday because he returned to Queensland, where he was employed, shortly afterwards. He brought a young Aboriginal girl from Queensland with him, who did all the housekeeping, cooking, shopping etc. Her name was Topsy and I thought she was very clever, especially when I saw her making soap in a big pot in the back garden! She also found time to teach me how to mend socks and I must have learnt my lesson well because, at quite an early age, I was earning the odd sixpence for darning the family's socks in quite a proficient manner.

We then lived in a rented house (now units) on the corner of Broadway and Ramsgate Streets, Glenelg. Mother decided she would never buy a house again, but before long she was going to auction sales and returning with a little table, a chair or two, some pieces of brass, and on one memorable occasion, when she made a bid for a collection of books, she was horrified to find it was a piano case full! And what books they were: the auction was at a wonderful old house called 'Stonehenge' in Partridge Street which had been owned by a family called Stonehouse. They must have been a highly educated family, as there were books in many languages and on all subjects. I still have a few on my shelves and one, which my parents gave to my youngest son Stephen, is a history of England written in 1660 – very bawdy English! With the spare room in our rented house rapidly filling with Mother's purchases, our parents decided that it was time perhaps to buy another house and finally bought one at 83 Augusta Street.

While we were still living on Broadway, I went for a few terms to a little private school, Miss Kingston's, so named for the woman and her mother who ran it. Mr Kingston, a company lawyer, bought three properties adjoining in Bristol Street, Glenelg; in one lived the boarders and the Kingstons, the middle one contained the class rooms, and the other was occupied by a Miss Dow, who had joined them in the venture. However, there was discussion between them and eventually, Miss Dow moved out and commenced her own school. The houses are still as they were, although considerably updated, and the school room section is a beautiful home with large rooms and, these days, a mezzanine floor where a master bedroom and bathroom have been added; it's only a few years since I last saw it (during an 'open for inspection' day) and for a minute I could imagine it all as it used to be, complete with blackboards, copy books and (believe it or not) dunces' caps. During recess period, we bought a penny bun at the little bakery on the corner that is now a delicatessen.

With the opening of an all-girls school, Woodlands, in Partridge Street, the little private schools – and there were several

– were forced to close. Both Joy and I attended Woodlands; I had commenced attendance before leaving Broadway and so continued to do so – though the walking distance was considerably longer – on moving to Augusta Street; Dick travelled by train, which at that time ran on the present tram route, to Pulteney Grammar School for Boys on South Terrace.

We had a happy childhood; our parents were devoted to each other, money was not particularly short, and as a family we enjoyed Sunday drives, picnics, pictures and the occasional holiday interstate. Mother and Dad loved playing cards, going to the theatre and (Mother at least) the horse races, where she seemed to have been lucky, rarely losing. She went alone, while we stayed home with Dad.

I don't ever remember enjoying my school days very much, though. I was shy, had absolutely no confidence in myself, and when scolded had an embarrassing habit of bursting into tears; I can remember, when realising that censure was inevitable, praying silently, that I WOULD be able to control the tears, but alas! it didn't work. Fortunately, I was mostly 'good'. I managed the schoolwork adequately – if not 'covering myself with glory' – and became an average tennis player. However, when I was selected to play in a tournament with spectators (other girls!), I went to pieces completely and hardly hit a ball. I hated sports days; I only had to think about 'not letting the team down' and I'd drop the ball, earning the scorn of my team mates – and I certainly couldn't run quickly, perhaps as a result of my weak ankles.

I DID have friends, though: Pauline Tolley, her sister Kath, and Mary Thompson. They all lived within a few minutes of our home so we were together a lot at weekends and after school. And with the beach and a tennis club almost at our front door, we didn't lack for entertainment or exercise during school vacations. The Tolley house in Second Avenue was where we seemed to be most, though; Mr and Mrs Cyril Tolley were the most hospitable couple, and with a family of four attractive daughters, the house was always full of young people playing Monopoly, Seven and a Half, and later Bridge. They seemed to love people, especially young people, coming to the house every Sunday night, singing around the piano, chatting by the fire or playing games.

In summer, their tennis court was a great attraction, and a walk to Glenelg to the sideshows, a stroll up the jetty or a ride around the Bay for a 'bob' in a motorboat, were all pleasant ways of spending a happy evening. Of course, when we had a 'heat wave', which as I remember it was pretty often, we would all meet on the beach at Kent Street, swimming and frolicking until late. On Sundays, we often went to St Peter's church; in the evenings, we'd meet a few choirboys and listen to the band on Colley Reserve or have a sundae at the kiosk on the end of the jetty. As we were all avid readers, the institute library had to be visited several nights a week; so safe was Glenelg in those days, that our parents had no qualms about allowing us to go and change books alone, nor did they have to worry about us should we take several hours to do so. In the pre-war years of which I am speaking, we had nothing to fear. Boys sometimes followed us home; there was a lot of giggling but that was all. Occasional cars tooted and the occupants would invite us to join them, but we just laughed about it all and were too well trained to think of getting into the car.

When I was sixteen, my brother Dick and I started going to the church younger-set dances on a Saturday night. These were a great success and very well attended; they were also well supervised and ended at a reasonable hour (so we had no excuse for not attending eight o'clock church in the morning!) although once a month they went on a little later. Many of the young people formed a group that we saw a lot at private parties and with whom we played tennis or made up Bridge parties. No one seemed to want to break into pairs; it was always as a crowd we did things. In later years, this sometimes happened, but not to me. My first steady boyfriend was an eighteen-year-old I met at Dick's twenty-first birthday; my parents had hired the supper room at the local town hall, a beautiful old building which is still very much in use. We danced and had the huge supper that was always mandatory, the inevitable speeches etc. I remember my mother had a beautiful black georgette dress made with little sequined cap sleeves and looked lovely and quite youthful. I probably didn't think so then, but when I look at old photographs now, I realise that such was the case. I remember I had on a red and white striped dress with a red sash and that I wasn't particularly happy in it. Nevertheless, I danced a lot with Bruce, who had accompanied his sister Ronda. Their surname was Quist and their older brother, Adrian, was a Davis Cup tennis player of repute. We met again at a tennis club dance – the Keswick Lawn Tennis Club, in fact. They always held their annual dance in summer and it was one of THE events. We danced on the lawn courts and, with a balmy night and soft lights, it certainly was a romantic atmosphere. From that night on, Bruce and I went out together steadily; he was blond and good-looking and I thought I was the luckiest and happiest girl in the world. Then it was pictures or dancing on Saturday nights and either tea at his home or tea at my house every Sunday night; we didn't see each other during the week days but there were 'phone calls, of course. As we didn't have much money in those days, and with only one car in the family, we mostly walked everywhere.

This happy state of affairs continued for fourteen months. Then I went on a holiday in Sydney and Melbourne with my parents and Joy; I remember we drove there in Dad's car, stopping several nights at little hotels on the way. I loved it but it was very hot, and as I have always suffered from car-sickness on windy roads, I was able to sit in front with Dad quite a lot of the time and that I loved. We stayed with our grandmother, Dad's mother, and several maiden aunts in Cremorne, and from there we visited old friends of Mother and Dad, and Auntie Elsie, Uncle George and their family. Auntie Elsie was Dad's eldest sister and as they had six children, it was quite a house full when we hit the place. The test cricket matches were on in Sydney; Dad and Mother were keen fans – Mother, of course, barracking (audibly!) for England.

Dad's brother Bob, his wife Belle (not quite accepted by the family because she was Catholic) lived next door to Grandma, with our cousins Graham and Gwen. I remember one beautiful balmy night when we walked across the Harbour Bridge to Luna Park.

Although, at nineteen, I was the eldest of the four of us, in those (sadly) past days, one had no need to fear anything, and nor did we. One of my great regrets is that my grandchildren don't have this freedom. However, as my wise little daughter Robin says, it doesn't matter because it's always been part of their lives to have a waiting parent outside the school gates, and delivering them and picking them up from other activities.

*

This is where Mum stopped writing. At some time or other, I must have read what she'd written and asked what had happened to Bruce, because in my hand, at the end of the above, I had written, 'Mum met a boy in Melbourne on the way home (his brother, Noel, liked Joy). They wrote to each other and he visited Adelaide.' Goodbye Bruce, I guess!

The Port Lincoln Years
1945–1966

Mum and Dad met at a football match shortly before the Second World War. He was olive-skinned, dark-haired, and cut a fine athletic figure on the field. She was brown-haired and fair-skinned and had a smile that engulfed her blue eyes.

By the time they married in Port Pirie on Christmas Eve 1941, Dad was a trainee pilot in the air force. Port Pirie was a small town near the top of Spencer's Gulf in South Australia; the air force base where Dad was stationed was close by. According to family folklore, it was 117 degrees in the shade the day they married, and given the tin-roofed church in which the ceremony was held, it was as brief as possible. They had a few days' honeymoon on Kangaroo Island – perhaps the only holiday they ever had alone – and then Dad returned to training and Mum to the lonely life of a war wife.

Their eldest child Richard was born in 1943 while Dad was serving in New Guinea. When the war ended, they moved to Port Lincoln, and it was there that four more children were born: Robin, me, John and, when Mum was forty-two, Stephen. Dad worked as a travelling salesman for the Mobil oil company, then as a tally clerk on the wharves, and finally as a clerk in the local branch of the Government Produce department.

Money was always short so Mum took in dressmaking and made curtains for Craven and Co., a local haberdashery and clothing store. She also helped make ends meet by growing vegetables for our dinner table. As a perk of Dad's job at the Government Produce department, he was given cheap meat for the family dog; when Mum discovered it was perfectly good gravy beef, we were fed lots of nourishing stews.

She was a good cook; her pasties were legendary and her mixed fruit and rolled-oats slice, Glug by name and nature, was a favourite with all our school friends. She was active on school welfare clubs and, with over sixteen years between the oldest and youngest of her children, once calculated that she'd baked about four hundred jubilee cakes for primary school cake stalls. (We won't even go into how many meringues, burnt-butter biscuits and stick-jaw toffees she made for the same cause.)

Despite the shortage of money and the workload involved in raising five children in a tiny government trust home, Mum always said she loved being a mother and that the Port Lincoln years were among her happiest.

117 degrees in the shade

It's Christmas Eve 1941, one of the hottest
December days on record. He's in air force
shirtsleeves, she's in blue-grey crêpe de Chine.
If he's a Clark Gable lookalike, she's June Allyson.
She's rolled her dark hair into a cluster of curls
and pinned them to the top her head.

They look happy. She set her heart early
but he's had to learn to put his jealousies aside,
to trust that though she might cameo with others,
he'll always be her leading man. So today,
with the world at war, while guarantees are few
and hopes are high, they're getting married.

His trust will be rewarded. Unlike Clark and June,
who never starred together, they'll have thirty-five years
of twin billing and gather about them a supporting
cast of five. Like Clark, his dark good looks
will slowly silver but, like Clark, years
of heavy smoking will end his life

before the credits are ready to roll.
She'll wait, like June, another thirty-five years
add ten grandchildren to the cast
(some great-grands as well) before she takes
her final bow, her hair a wisp of white cloud
pinned to the top of her head.

Flashback

Flashback seventy years to a country hospital
where a woman, my mother,
is left alone to get on with it
while Sister lends a hand on the ward.

But soon, too soon, she feels the baby coming
and pushes the call button that no one hears.
And pushes again.　　　　And again.
And still no one comes.
So there, in that converted kitchen,
with no one to hear the laboured wrenching
of new life from within her own,
she gives birth to a daughter, my sister
who lies uncomplaining in the chill of late July
for twenty minutes before my mother,
frantically trying to keep her warm but fearful
of suffocation, alerts a passerby
who alerts the Sister　　　who alerts the doctor
who says, 'Put her out and I'll stitch her up.'
And they do.　　And he does.

And later when my sister won't eat
and her hands hang like broken wings,
and later still when she can't do her sums
and the teacher smacks her
and still she can't do her sums,
it's too late and my mother says,
'That's life. They were busy.
People make mistakes.'

And no one's heard of negligence.
Or million-dollar lawsuits.
Except maybe the doctor.
Who waives his bill.　　Just this once.

Picture

The frame is adjustable. You can draw it tight around the girl
and the concrete pipeline, cool against her legs, where she sits
making dandelion chains. You can lift it up and open it out
to encompass a pale patch of sky above her head,
and the sea plying its pitiless trade behind her.

Sometimes, sketch it in around the bulk of a 1937
Willys Knight, its bonnet up, the girl's father
staring into its depths, hoping to spot the two and two
that might make four and with a single turn of the crankshaft,
wrench the engine into life again.

At other times, tuck it in around the girl, her brother and sister
stalking the dandelions for those with the thickest stems,
bending them over and snapping them off,
making a clean thumbnail incision near the base,
then threading them, one through the other, until each flower
sits snug against the stem of the next.

One day, in expansive mood, choose a different frame,
something filmic and fanciful to hold the father
wiping grease from a smile of astonished satisfaction;
the mother, hair rolled into curls and pinned to the top
of her head, turning round from the front seat to admire
the dandelions and regale the children
with the pissabeds of old English folklore.

Let it show the girl running behind a tree,
returning with the back of her dress caught in her knickers;
then the car, shuddering with the shock of newfound grace,
carrying them off down a country road.

Chopping the wood

Up there in the shantung sky, among
the shivering stars, the man in the moon,
axe poised like a promise above his head,

chopped the wood that set the night ablaze.
I'd stare unblinking until my eyes watered
for fear of missing the moment –

any time now –
when he would swing through
and slice his world in two.

Down here, it was our mother
in dressing gown and slippers,
hair slipping from its clips and combs,

who stumbled out in the morning light
to chop the wood
that kept the kitchen range alight.

Each thunk! from the axe, each woodchip ping!
as it hit the fence, was another cake or batch
of biscuits, a Sunday roast or rabbit stew.

In the winter months, she draped my socks
over the fireguard to dry off in time for school –
except for once when, the wood wet, refusing to catch,

she tucked them in the cleft of her bosom.

23 Tennant Street

While we were at Sunday school singing
of bright and beautiful things and wondering
how the dropping pennies would be delivered
to Jesus up there in the clouds (and who knew
there were shops in heaven?),

our parents were cutting back the roses,
redirecting the nasturtiums to their designated
corner by the front fence, freshening up
the purple pansy patch, and setting to rights
the stones that bordered the beds, dislodged
(again) by a spirited game of rounders
or chasey, red rover or hide-and-seek.

Whatever faith the day instilled came not
from the little wooden church at the top
of the street but from our parents who we knew
would be there when we got home – muddy
kneed, up to their wrists in pansy planting,
and not altogether pleased to see us so soon –

but there.

Making do

I'm sitting on the baby bentwood beside the fire
darning my school socks, sending a row
of lifelines from one side of a gaping hole
to the other, then weaving the wool in
and out to create a neat bed of threads.

My mother is sitting next to my sister.
When she isn't picking up my sister's dropped
knitting stitches, or threading my needle again,
she's reading to us: *Mary Jones and her Bible*,
my Sunday school attendance prize.
It's a story of poverty, of making do; of Mary,
gathering firewood to sell for a farthing until
she has twenty-four and can walk twenty-five
barefoot miles to buy her very own Bible.

Soon, my mother will push her feet back
inside her slippers, go out to the cold kitchen,
and finding the cake cupboard bare, take out
the battered saucepan that belonged to her mother,
set it on the kitchen range (still hot from cooking
dinner) and with butter, sugar, cocoa and milk,
make some chocolate fudge.

She'll pile it onto a plate, smooth it into shape
and cut it into squares. 'Let's wait till it's cool!' she'll say.
But lacking Mary's will and patience, we'll count to ten
and scoff the lot.

Skittles

The numbers
in my mother's
dressmaking
book were
the vital
statistics
of the matriarchs
in our small town.
A quick scan of its pages
and we knew whose big-bosomed
frontage could cut a swathe among
the main street shoppers and who
required a wide berth behind; small
children were skittles in a bowling
alley should one such rear-end en-
dowed bend to retrieve a dropped
coin or key. And in an age when
teachers were hard-edged and rock-
jawed as Easter Island monoliths,
only I knew my grade seven teacher
was courting a 'bust' at all, let alone
38 inches of it squashed flat as two
trapped bundles of newborn naked-
ness by her buttoned-to-the-neck
blouses and double-breasted wool-
len jackets. Our spelling mistakes
rose in strangulated sighs like
bad news from the barricade.

The wharfie, the dressmaker and the fifth child

Late one night in August
when there were no ships to unload
and no seams to unpick
and the three-year-old's asthmatic rattle
had eased to the wheeze of a toy underfoot,

they crept hand-in-hand to the laundry
and between white rollers
and stifled laughter,
in a watery light wrung out from the moon,
they placed the contraceptive tube.

He turned the handle
while she, her hands a chalice,
scooped up the exiguous offering
and with two fingers and wanton smile,
thrust it high between her thighs.

Later that night
when his ship came in
it met an unresisting tide
and cells began dividing,
seamless as the sea.

Coffin Bay

On the day our parents went out in the boat and didn't come back,
we walked along the shaded path where the tiny eyelets of light
from overhanging trees were all I knew of enchantment then
and all I know now. And when we came to the shop, we bought
blue iceblocks in square cones and sucked the sweetness
to the backs of our throats where hard lumps of fear
had risen like gelatin in home-made ice cream.
Then we walked along the water's edge as if it were the edge
of our lives, and gazed out to sea and thought of killer whales
that drape themselves in seaweed and lie in wait for stray seals
then take them in their mouths and toss them and bat them
from one end of the bay to the other until they're tenderised
and ready for eating – except for one which they ferry back to shore
and place gently on the sand.
And we thought of those seals and willed that our parents
would be amongst the chosen; that the changing tides that took them
would change again, and ferry them back to shore,
and lay them at our feet. Then out in the bay a boat appeared
with three smaller boats trailing along behind. And in the last of them
were our parents, our mother sitting in the stern as still and serene
as the figurehead from a long-forgotten ship.
And we ran along the beach and skimmed a few stones
and got back in time for tea.

Mum and Uncle Bob

Sometimes, we'd come home from school
and she'd be at the sewing machine, a grey-haired
madonna stitching a heavenly cloud of the pink or green
or midnight blue of the town's annual ballet concert.
Uncle Bob would be sitting on the other side
of the kitchen table, a cup of tea gone cold
at his elbow, smoke rising from a cigarette
that we never saw him light nor ever stub out.

Her face would be flushed like a schoolgirl's –
partly the effort of pushing yards and yards
of stiffened tulle beneath the two-toed foot
of the sewing machine, partly the ease and irresistible
pull of words that flowed back and forth across
the table. Books, films, and the life of the mind
sparked her imagination, rescued it from the stress
and tedium of home detention when ends
were distant and never looked like meeting.

Dad loved her and she loved him, but Uncle Bob
was the keeper of her flame, and if once or twice
it threatened a wildfire fit to burn the house down,
there was always the cold water of our arrival home
from school to douse the embers and wave away
the whispers of love on the wrong side.

In the early evenings then,

we were a tumble of kids littering
the lounge room floor with tomboy stitch
and scrounged wool, knucklebones still gristled
with sheep, and three-storey card houses
lickspittled to make them stick.

Our mother, pink-cheeked by the fire,
turned our tomboys into pot holders,
and soothed frayed tempers when the huff
and puff from the front door slamming
blew the card house down.

Our work-and-weather-worn father bought
forgiveness for one more round at the pub,
with a bulging bag of mixed lollies for us
and marshmallow novelties – inexplicably
shaped like guns – for our mother.

When our tongues had searched out
morsels of mint or musk held hostage in hideouts
between our teeth, we'd gaze up at our mother,
(who knew to make things last) her lips poised
around the barrel of a marshmallow gun.

Tiddalik

My mother gives me my brother's medicine,
remembers I'm allergic to penicillin.

Doesn't wait for me to swell like Tiddalik,
sit in a corner, quietly croak. Rings the doctor.

Give her bicarb, he says. Make her sick, he says.
I'm fourteen. Being sick is inelegant. I refuse.

My parents shout, argue. With me, with each other.
I begin to feel cold, clammy. My finger pads swell.

My father gives me salt water, 50% proof.
Warns of escapees from makeshift ponds

found splay-legged and dry as old shoe leather,
in amongst the dust balls, under the bed.

I stick two fingers down my throat.
Bring up the ocean, a couple of rivers.

My mother supplies the rest in tears.

The Twelve Days of Christmas

Classroom Visiting Day, December 1960

Just as you arrive at the classroom door,
a gallinaceous game bird takes up the tune

and with the merest riffling of its pear tree,
leads us through a merry chase

of all manner of beaked creatures,
not least of them the in fact beakless

five gold rings of the matrimonial genus.
And in the wake of seven swans swimming

come eight cows, all of them *udderly* invisible
were it not for the milkmaids sitting squat by their sides.

And by the time the ladies of the manor
are being reeled away in a flurry of frog-like gallantry

with the song going on   and on
you have to leave and have no time

to witness the unwavering rule of my margins
or the interlocking curlicues of my Grade Five flourish.

And though I now give short shrift to true love
and the repetitive tokenism

of anything resembling it,
I think often of the feathered wisp of your hat

and the elegant clip-clip of your black stilettos
as you hurried away to another of your brood

and of how you always were
the very centre of our paradise.

Return to Adelaide
1966

My brother John, the fourth of Mum and Dad's children and the second youngest, was a bad asthmatic and continually hospitalised. In between times, Mum did all she could to keep him breathing – whether that involved another batch of the 'witch's brew' she made from slippery elm powder and Spanish liquorice, or sheer will alone. But with no signs of long-term improvement, the decision was made to move from the asthma-exacerbating wheat fields surrounding Port Lincoln, to suburban Adelaide and its greater accessibility to medical specialists.

Education was also a deciding factor: as children of the Great Depression and unable to complete their education because of it, Mum and Dad were determined that their children be allowed to pursue their education and career prospects as far as they wanted, no matter the added financial burden it would entail. Tertiary education had already made it necessary for their oldest child, Rick, to live in Adelaide, and it wouldn't be long before others of their brood would need to do the same.

Meanwhile, the added stress of caring for a dangerously ill child had taken its toll and in 1966, a few months before we moved to Adelaide, Mum suffered a stroke. It left her with a short-term memory disability, and us with a lifetime of having to repeat ourselves or stop everything to help her find her glasses, her chequebook, her shoes – whatever it was that she'd put down a minute or two before but could no longer remember where. A small price to pay for her continued presence in our lives, and in every other way, she carried on as before: dressmaking, cooking for a friend's homemade cake shop, and making curtains for a local company – anything to help keep us all clothed and fed.

Dad had his health problems too. Asthmatic like John, he had been a heavy smoker for many years. Emphysema, the inevitable result, forced an early retirement in his late fifties, but with his veteran's pension and Mum's carer allowance, they had more income than ever before. More importantly, the cost of educating their two youngest children (the others having already left home for travel or work or marriage purposes) was guaranteed.

The education entitlement didn't stop in 1976 when Dad died, but the pensions did. The war widows pension – when it finally came through after months of no income at all – meant a return to the financial impossibility of feeding and housing herself and two teenagers, and it wasn't until she was sixty and eligible for the age pension that Mum was able to relax the purse strings a little.

Mum was devastated when Dad died and missed him for the rest of her life. There were a few widowers hanging around at various times – Mum was always a very elegant woman and great company. But none of them could quite equal Dad. Paul Newman or Sean Connery might have fitted the bill at a pinch but, sadly for them, they were busy elsewhere.

Stroke

While we were standing around
salted and sandy
after a day spent fishing
and she was cooking the catch,
her brain was hatching an ischemic plot –

a clot – that would force the banks
of a blood vessel to burst
and plunge her
into a place of not knowing:
where she was or who she was.

Even her children's names had gone.
Each of us in turn drawn to her bedside
to trigger a response, her eyes alighted
on the fourth of her five-strong brood.
'My little Johnny-cake,' she said.

The relief of her return was immediate,
but for us to feel secure enough
for sibling rivalry to set its
shameless course again,
took a little longer:

Why him and not me?

After the stroke,

it was enough that all our names returned,
that she could set them correctly
beside each shining face, like naming flowers
in a botany exam. So when she couldn't remember
where we'd been or where we were going,

though we told her over and over, we learned
not to cast our eyes to the heavens or buffet her
with our sighs. And one day, when she lost
her chequebook (again) and sent us in search,
we treated it as a game

and sent progress reports back down the line:
Your missing shoe in the backyard shed, Mum!
Last week's shopping list in the cutlery drawer!
Is this your shrivelled head under the bed, Mum?
She found the chequebook herself,

on the floor in front of her chair,
under her left foot. We laughed, and ever after,
whenever one of us lost anything – passport,
car keys, (a kilo or two) – we joked about
the kleptomaniacal tendencies of her left foot.

Card sharp

'Let's play Racing Patience,' she'd say.
We'd agree and sit in a circle on the floor, each
with our pack of cards and private will to win.

Her fingers were nimble, her eyes sparked
a determined blue light, she put her cards down
with lightning speed and a stinging slap

and we were not three minutes
into the game before we realised
that her will to win was ten times ours.

Her hard work and self-sacrifice
had given us the education that she,
as a child of the depression and a girl at that,

had been denied. This, this skill as a card sharp,
this chance to crow – 'I won! Don't they teach you
anything these days?' – she would keep for herself.

Photograph: Mum on a South Pacific cruise, 1977

Here she is, elegant in navy and white,
on board the SS *Arcadia* as it leaves Sydney.
Behind her, the sails of the Opera House
are scooping out a chunk of sky.
A moment before, she was marvelling
at their design, all those interlocking tiles…
Now her friend, Jean, has brought her round
to take a snap – *Quick, before they slide by!*

How happy she looks: thirty-four years
of child-rearing and the home-grown
hand-me-down habits of feeding and clothing
a family of seven on money enough for three,
are over; the children are making their own way
and now, with a generous birthday cheque
from family members, and the relative wealth
of her war widow's pension, it's her turn.

For her sake, for the romantic heart she never lost,
I'd like to think she had a glad eye for the captain
when he joined their table at dinner; that he
was equally entranced and led her round
the dance floor more times than was seemly
for a married man; that she went to bed that night
wishing a tryst had been possible – if she
were that kind of girl, if he were that kind of man.

But if none of that happened, there was always Jean,
whose risqué sense of humour, like her breasts
in a too-small swim-suit in the Sydney surf
the day before, could not be contained.
And now that I've enlarged the photo,
it's unmistakable: my mother's eyes
are crinkling up and a teasing admonition
is itching to break free: 'Oh Jean!'

Triple trounced

She left school at fourteen but when our mother's mind
wasn't *Webster's Dictionary*, or *Miss Manner's Book
of Common Courtesy*, it was a Letraset jumble of letters
that spent part of each day falling in and out with each other:
> three-letter words beginning with 'a',
> seven-letter words that housed a 'z',
> four-letter words with no need for an 'e'.

On rainy days, the Scrabble board emerged
and we'd no sooner placed the three-letter
Nip-and-Fluff word we'd spent ten minutes excavating
from a dictionary already bloodied with our desperation,
> than she would trounce it
> with a 'j' on a triple-letter
> or a 'z' on the double-word.

When she reached the finishing line,
she'd look back at us – trailing our degrees
and advanced diplomas where she had none –
see that we were held to ransom
> by four 'a's
> or a 'v'
> or a 'u'-less q

and not even try to stifle a smile.

After falling from a car on the way home from the Teachers' Ball

I'm sitting opposite my mother. Between us
on the table, is her sewing machine and the ruched

and riven no-man's-land of my torn dress.
She takes up the ragged edges, pins them together,

clamps them beneath the two-taloned claw
of the sewing machine. She pushes her knee hard

against the lever, closes the rent with a battery
of stitches, bites the thread and releases the dress.

I touch the tender wound that cuts a jagged course
down the side of my face.

She pulls the pin from her mouth, leans forward,
and fires the words that inadvertently scar the breast

of a plain house brown that already doubts its worth:
'Did you fall? Or were you pushed?'

The Letters

Before Skype and Facebook and email, when long-distance phone calls were expensive or difficult or scratchy with static, there were letters. My mother's letters to me while I was travelling, or living in Israel, or teaching in country South Australia, were accounts of her life in suburban Adelaide. My letters to her and Dad were accounts of the places I saw and the people I met – and not as frequent as they would have liked. But occasionally, letters lent themselves to the disclosing of matters that other daughters may not have wanted – or felt able – to tell their mothers. And her letters in return were equally candid.

In 1976, the year of Dad's death, I took up a teaching post in Loxton, in South Australia's Riverland. I stayed there for twenty years; during that time, I married, had two children and, after thirteen years of marriage, divorced. It is during those years that most of the letters from my mother that I still have were written. Only some of the letters have been included in this book, and often only in excerpt form. But the many hours I spent rereading and typing them all were a total pleasure.

Reading Mum's letters

Gone now these past several years,
many more since she wrote these letters,
yet here she is in every line –
a wonder that the ink is dry.
Each word rings like a struck bell
with her voice, her inflection,
like listening to a recording
with the sound turned down.
That she's not sitting opposite me
as I read is more the miracle
than if I were to look up and see her
sipping her coffee and regarding me
with the blue blessing of her eyes,
ready to tell the back stories
that spilled beyond the bounds of letters
or had dug in deeper than even the trowel
of pen and ink could unearth.

23rd June 1972

Our Dear Lou,

I thought of you yesterday and hoped you had a happy day – of course my mind flew back to the cold June day you were born – helped along by Dr Clarkson – and how Auntie Marge Ross left her class to their own devices for a while, and came up to see me with a bunch of flowers – I think she even raced Dad! – strangely enough I picked up the paper today and there was a photo of Dr Clarkson with his two brothers – he arrived back from US yesterday and was installed as Governor of Rotary last night…

Dad is coming home today – the doctor wanted him to stay another week, but Dad convinced him the hospital wasn't doing anymore than he could do at home, and he IS feeling better, he says. I'm afraid he's going to find the cold weather a bit trying though – yesterday was the coldest day for four years – and the ward was kept heated all the time with strip radiators on the walls. Still we'll see. They've also got him doing postural drainage (like John used to do).

I suppose you've gathered that I'm having a day off work today (Friday) and as usual I am scribbling this in bed – much the warmest place with the blanket switched on. I also had Wednesday off. Robin spent the day here and I tried to get her coat made. She needs it badly, but as it's black (with red lining), I can't see to sew it at night. I made quite a lot of headway, but had to leave it to go to the shopping centre and then to the doctor's – just the usual checkup and more prescriptions. My blood pressure is down and the mole on my back which Auntie Joy tut-tutted about, is quite alright – so much for that…

We've just received another letter from you and have enjoyed reading a further episode in your happy life on a kibbutz – I still feel I'd love it myself but can't quite see Dad without his TV and *The World of Sport*...

Much love and cheer Louise,

From your famille

Mama, Papa et frères

(So much for your Hebrew – try my French!)

27th July 1972

Dear Louise,

Thank you for your letters – received earlier this week – we are very grateful for the frequency of them.

You sounded happy about your change of employment and I can see that the open air life would be a pleasant change after the cooking odours and chores of the kitchen – sorry you felt Ralph's departure so keenly – no perhaps I'm not – caring for someone is not something to regret – it's all part of life, and a good part. It would be much sadder never to care enough about anyone. Anyway, you'll probably meet again sometime – I've always found that people usually 'bob' up again later on. However the important thing is not to 'pine' but just get on with living and making more friends – you seem to be collecting plenty, and from all parts of the world and this is good...

27th March 1973

Our Dear Louise,

We were all delighted to receive your most welcome and interesting letters last week – your trip around Israel sounds fascinating, your 'end of session' breakup quite hilarious and of course we're ever so proud of your good reports – such clever children we have!…

I'm sure I've told you before but I repeat again, if you need some money we can manage to send you some without any hardship – not thousands of course but enough to see you through a spell in London if that's what you want to do – we've also offered to pay off the last $300 or so of Rick's bond, so just remind him to let us know where we should pay it and to whom…

It is now Wednesday 28th March. Today Dad and I had an appointment with a man at Repat – about pensions etc – quite painless and encouraging, especially that the boys' education is assured, even up to tertiary level – on through tertiary level I should say. John can do his librarian course full time at university and get a living allowance to boot – I imagine this is a great help to Dad's morale – and should be some encouragement to the boys. The boys also had an interview last week.

Our Repat appointment was at eleven o'clock so I had plenty of time to go to a luncheon and mannequin parade at a church hall at Brighton – the clothes came from an exclusive frock shop in Brighton but were all a bit beyond my modest budget – afterwards Joy (who sold me the ticket) and I went to Marion – Joy is apparently in need of winter clothes. So am I but I think I'll start making something – anyway we didn't find anything inspiring.

The weather turned cold during last night and we've been shivering today – quite a shock to the system to have the maximum temperature at midnight and then wake to a really cold morning, but I'm hoping I'll develop a little more energy. At present I seem to work on a day on, day off system – a busy day Monday and then I've 'had it' all the following day. Do you think I'm getting old?!...

I'll have to finish this my dear Lou. David Frost is interviewing Paul Newman tonight and that I must see. David Frost has been doing a series of interviews with some of the better known film stars – already I've seen Sophia Loren (she was terrific – natural, charming and beautiful) and Shirley MacLaine who is apparently an adventurous type – climbs mountains etc...

29th March 1973

...Paul Newman was NOT a disappointment – well-spoken, intelligent, interested in everything – not a bit conceited or anxious to talk about himself. Even with David Frost asking the questions, he managed to avoid anything of too personal a nature and is much better looking than in his pictures. Sorry about the way I rave on, ME at my age, but I'm always delighted when someone I've admired doesn't disappoint me...

13th November 1974

My Dear Louise,

As you said in your letter I had guessed as to its contents, but I'm so glad you at last found it necessary to tell me. I must be honest and say it saddens me, but after quite a lot of thought, I must also be honest and say that given the same opportunities, freedom and independence I might have behaved in much the same way. Anyway I certainly don't feel any less love for you, I am certainly not disgusted – just terribly worried that you are going to be 'hurt' by it all. I should hate – like hell – to see you go from one affair to another until you become completely blasé about everything. I can't blame you kids for not thinking too highly of marriage, but I still think it's the only basis on which to bring up children, and since my own children have given me so much happiness – I don't think we'd have lasted two years without them! – I'd not like to think you could be deprived of similar happiness…

…to be honest, I'm also glad I've not got frigid daughters – so many are, even these days, and in my generation it was almost considered indecent to admit to enjoying 'that side of marriage' as it was so delicately put – frankly, I found it all very 'decent'!…

Meanwhile – DON'T neglect your teaching commitments please – if you only knew how I've wished I had a career to occupy me of latter years.

Much love – as always
M.O.M.*

7th March 1975

…Dad is having tests again at Daws Road Hospital – blood tests last week and I think it's more X-rays next week. His loss of weight seems the main concern…

---

* When I was four and my sister eight, we were sent around the corner to post a letter. On the way home, a couple of older boys teased us: 'Mad old Duffys!' they called out. But the Duffys were the people next door; we were the Atkinsons. So I set them straight. 'We're not the mad old Duffys. We're the mad old Atkinsons!' A friend of our family's called us 'the M.O.A.s' ever after, and Mum often signed her letters to her children as M.O.M. – Mad Old Mum.

3rd February 1976

My Dear Louise,

Delighted to receive a letter from our poor little homeless waif! Do hope you aren't sleeping under a tree – or worse! – and that your next letter will have happier news of the accommodation situation. We'll also be anxious to hear how the new school and teaching staff are compared with the Whyalla version. No doubt it will be a bit of a trauma for a while, but at least you seem to have a friend already in Starr…

I've not been very well lately and the checkup at the doctors last week had my blood pressure even higher. However, it's gone back to normal again now although I'm still on antibiotics to try and 'fix' my facial pains. Dr Boorman says it's a sinus infection – whatever, I had very little sleep for a week in spite of sleeping pills, but I'm hoping I'll be alright soon…

This is such a dull, boring letter and I wish it were otherwise. But I'm afraid nothing very exciting is ever going to happen to me again – at least that's how I feel today. (It's probably just the antibiotics depressing me so don't let it worry you too much.)…

Have you read *Paradise* by Patrick Dennis? John got it from the library and I'm quite enjoying it. I'm now reading one of Patrick White's, alternating it with *Fear of Flying* which was suggested reading at Delta* – but I'm getting heartily bored with THAT four letter word which seems to appear in practically every paragraph. Incidentally, I think Erica Jong, who you may remember is the authoress, is coming here for the Festival of Arts.

Dad is about the same, but has taken to sitting up later – retires to the bedroom to get his coughing fit over with and then

---

* Delta, from memory (Google being unforthcoming in this instance), was a women's reading and discussion group.

comes back again for some more of the wonderful entertainment being dished up on the TV!…

Think I'll do a little sewing – do hope you are well our Lou – I'll try to make my next letter full of 'joie de vivre'.

Much love from us all,

M.O.M.

11th February 1976

Our Dear Louise,

How's this for a prompt reply? Only received your letter this morning and here I am. It was so nice to have some more news of you and to know that the school, air conditioning and headmaster all meet with your approval. Only hope that the accommodation situation clears up soon too…

We – Dick, Joy and I – have moved Nana to another nursing home this morning. The new one is Miroma just near Daws Road Repat Hospital – an easy distance for Joy to manage (unlike Reynella) and more convenient for me, too. It is, or was, a doctor's home, and hasn't that squeaky clean institutional air that Reynella had. She is sharing a large bedroom, and the furniture and beds are NOT the hospital type. There is also a lovely garden and a big verandah – I only hope she can settle down happily there and doesn't give them a bad time. Reynella didn't seem too reluctant to lose her especially since she 'escaped' again on Saturday! Joy was all 'churned up' (her expression, not mine) over the whole thing and when she left here was trying to decide if she should go out on a lunch date, feeling so miserable! Me – I only wished I had a lunch date to go to! I'm beginning to get a bit bored lately – after all the people around at Christmas and early in the new year, life has settled down to the old routine. No more Bridge to break up the week and I haven't enough energy to garden, to clean out cupboards or even take much interest in the housework! Thank heavens Delta started again yesterday and we're doing another of Patrick White's books, *Riders in the Chariot*, which I'm enjoying immensely…

26th February 1976

Our Dear Lou,

Thank you for your TWO welcome letters – very pleased we were, and it's sorry I am not to have written immediately. Really meant to, but Delta on Tuesday, Bridge yesterday and Nana in between times, to say nothing of the trouble I'm still having with my face – on occasions – and the hot weather! Well I know you'll get the picture…

7th March 1976

…Dad has been in bed all day today – feels worse than usual but doesn't quite know why. I guess I have to expect that he'll gradually get worse since there is no chance of any improvement…

I'm going to a choral evening in St Peters Cathedral tomorrow night with Lale Dollard – Delta on Tuesday and Bridge on Wednesday. It's going to be difficult as my face is still giving me hell – except when I keep my mouth shut! The doctor still says it's arthritis aggravated by tension and anxiety. Perhaps I should 'get me to a nunnery' – with a vow of silence of course! – but all the things I enjoy involve some movement of the jaw! Time for tea – much love, Lou. Steve joins in this, so does Dad.

25th April 1976
Anzac Day

My Dear Lou,

Sorry I've not written before this but it's been a busy week and, as you know, I'm a bit handicapped with this arthritis in my leg – at least that's what the doctor says and since there's no cure as yet, I just have to learn to live with it, I guess. Actually, if I keep busy and warm, don't eat any sweet things and try to relax as much as possible, it's really not too bad. I have a little book I bought from the health shop last year that I've only just read, and it says that arthritis is often at its most painful stage just after one has lost a spouse! Incredible isn't it?*

But enough of that! I hope you had a pleasant relaxing weekend and are coping well with your little 'hopefuls'. Only a few weeks and you can have your well-earned two weeks remission for good behaviour. Are you planning to go somewhere exciting or are you coming home?

I've finally sorted out Dad's insurance policy – thanks to Keith Bolitho who met me in Adelaide on Friday. I signed papers and documents, produced the marriage license to prove I was the widow mentioned in Dad's will etc etc and finally they agreed to pay the money into my bank account. I now have to go through another series of papers to get the car registered in my name. Honestly it's ridiculous and I can't apply for a widow's pension until I've been widowed for six weeks! Don't ask me why!...

I was still in bed when Rob rang this morning (they have the phone on now) to ask us to go for a drive to Myponga. Rob took lunch and we ate it on the seafront. I enjoyed getting out

---

* Dad had died at home on 1 April.

and the countryside was lovely. The kids were good and except that John slipped down a sand hill and sat in something rather unpleasant and had to put his trousers in the boot and come home in his underpants, a good time was had by all. Larissa in her rush to tell us about it got somewhat confused – as she put it 'Johnnie just dogged in the poo!'...

Much love to you, my dear Lou, as always
M.O.M.

19th July 1976

...Rob said you and Starr are coming down for the Bolshoi Ballet? Let me know when, and I'll make a grand gesture – like vacuuming the carpets, cleaning the stove and maybe even defrosting the fridge. Actually I'm going to the ballet, too, with Aileen Dollard. She's going to try for tickets to *Anna Karenina* on the Saturday night – I'm hoping that's also the night and ballet you want to see.

The phone bill arrived today and I'm still in a state of shock. I don't think I can let you pay it all, but I've got a fortnight to think about it...

25th July 1976

...I am half watching *Wuthering Heights* while I'm writing this – it's years since I saw it and even longer since I read the book. The photography, colour etc are excellent, but no one could play Heathcliff like Lawrence Olivier...

Can hardly keep awake tonight – didn't sleep well last night – so I'll say 'Goodnight' with much love – as always,
M.O.M.

20th September 1976

My Dear Lou,

So happy I am for you! Fancy getting that Italian course! Hope you also get the part in the play so I can visit Loxton and see you 'tread the boards'. Glad the Israeli talk was successful too – not that I doubted it would be.

Probably just as well you missed out on the driving test – I felt that the few weeks you've been practising were hardly enough for a lifetime of driving. You'll probably get it next time anyway. I can understand how anxious you must be to be independent of other people's transport – I should dearly like to be able to take myself to places too. It's also a means of escape when the house is a bit confining – and I'm sure that's what it will be to you – or rather what it already is.

I felt a bit flat (unfortunately not anatomically!) when you left and the boys returned to their educational pursuits, and THAT worried me as I have no desire to be a dependent. All the same, I guess I do need company – I'm no loner. However, I managed to fill last week with Delta, a morning tea at the Freemason's village, babysitting for Bilha and Rick, visiting Nana and Auntie Alice, a hurried trip to the pictures one morning to see *A Touch of Class* for the third time! – John hadn't seen it – some sewing and turning out of drawers and Robin, Larissa and Antony here on Friday with Mookie and the twins adding to the ménage in the afternoon while Rick took Bilha to the doctor for another check-up (all is well)…

The boys are well and Stephen seems to be keener to pass since his art teacher praised his painting and said if he could submit two more of the same standard, he had a good chance of a credit in Art! He says now he's going to get his Matric and since he usually puts a spurt on in the last term I can only hope he's right.

Robin and the children are well – Roger always is – likewise the Richard Atkinsons. The twins are delightful – Nitsan grows more beautiful and has the blackest hair, and Gilli is smiling all the time. So lucky I am to have a beautiful batch of grandchildren as well as five beautiful children – I should be ashamed of my fits of depression – and I am – but I still seem to get taken over by them from time to time. I guess it's always been like that.

Must start some housework –
Much love to you, my dear Lou
M.O.M. and the boys

28th October 1976

My Dear Lou, so nice to get a letter
Glad to say that I'm feeling much better
The boys are well and full of fun,
But there's always work they haven't done.
Steve's second painting is very good,
But where's number three? – he has the wood –
Since there must be at least one more
I worry a lot, you can be sure.
Next Wednesday Larissa will be just four
You'd better remember or she'll get sore,
We're going up to a Birthday tea
Just Auntie Joy, Mookie & me.
Last Sunday we had Rick and Bilha to lunch
The kids came too – we had the whole bunch
Those twins are really quite delightful

If they go away it will be quite frightful.
Mookie too, is very good,
And always behaves just as she should.
Glad to hear the play went well
Didn't doubt it would truth to tell…
…Writing like this takes no time at all
But pretty soon it's bound to pall
You must try it sometime, it's lots of fun
But for you there's always so much to be done
Must stop this now and get some tea
May write more later – I'll have to see.

29th October 1976

Most of last night I sat and sewed
I've still lots to do – there's such a load!
I'll be glad when it's all finished and done
Perhaps then there'll be time to just sit in the sun.
So lovely it is in the sun today,
I wouldn't do anything could I have my way.
But pretty soon, Rob will be arriving,
And I'll be caught, so I'd best be showering.
Remember me to those around you,
And love to you my little Lou.

November 1976

Dear little Lou, How are you?
And your little Honda? Going well, I wonda (?)
I'm still in bed. Have a cold in the head
But I'm much better so I'm writing this letter,

Haven't been out – it's been quite a bout,
But some curtains I've made – hope I get paid!
The machine has run hot, so much sewing I've got.
How is the play? Or can't you quite say?
And what of the dancing? Can just see you prancing.
Are you watching your weight? I have been – of late!
I hope you take care and of strangers beware,
Keep your car doors locked, then you won't get socked,
John is still sleeping – such hours he is keeping!
Stephen has a cold, or so I am told,
Think he is shamming – his results will be damning
He's strumming his guitar – such a noise! Wah-wah-wah!…
Must get up I suppose and start washing the clothes.
Remember me to your friend Starr and love to you – your loving Ma.

(Undated)

A Pome
To Thee from Me (undated)
Dear Lou and Phil, I really will
Write more often in future
But the time goes by, the days just fly
So it's just a note – will that suit you?
The trip in the bus will be fun for us
A few days away from work,
(I have English to finish and work to diminish
And other things I can't shirk)
But see you we will, it will be quite a thrill
Will the patrons throw posies of flowers?
Will they pour lots of wine? Give you programmes to sign
After standing in line for hours?
Will you be busy for days, rehearsing for plays

Or staying on location?
Will you no longer teach but relax on the beach
The darling of the whole nation.
But it's only just fun, there's work to be done
I'm just a proud old Mum
It will soon be high noon, so we'll see you both soon,
(I know you'll be glad when we come)
So it's love and best wishes and back to the dishes
With love and kisses
Mum

P.S. On a saner note, the bus leaves at 5.45 Friday evening. Perhaps Phil shouldn't see this – or he'll KNOW we're all 'nuts'.
    M.O.M.

29th July 1981

'Pomeforlu'
Write me a pome my little Lou said,
So here I am (I should be OUT of bed!)
I should be dressing – it's Bridge today,
and anyway, I'm guessing there's not much to say.
Robin and Roger are still away
It was cold and grey all yesterday.
John is 'flat out' now he's back at school,
so it's dinner and bed as a general rule.
Stephen came in – he wanted some ink –
he looks lean and hungry I always think.
Tonight's the Royal Wedding* – I bet she looks delightful –
Only hope nothing happens – wouldn't that be frightful?

* Prince Charles married Lady Diana Spencer.

So glad the strikes are over, though I wasn't the least affected,
but one sometimes wonders if their brains should be dissected!
Can't they see the cost of food will just go on rising.
At least that's the way it seems to go (I'm not just surmising)
It's really so cold and I MUST get up,
but perhaps of coffee I'll have a cup.
It's really so cold and I don't know what to wear –
my sister and I are quite a pair!
She has too much and can't make a decision
while most of my wardrobe should go to the Mission!
One of these days I'll start over from scratch.
I'll have six of everything and of course they'll all match!
But meanwhile I'll arise and find me a dress.
It will no doubt look better if I give it a press.
So it's goodbye to you both with love and good wishes.
Gosh! It's late! I must do the dishes!
(Not my best effort but the best I can do –
I only had a minute or two!) M.O.M.

Room 31
Ward 19
(Undated)

My Dear Lou – a poem for you,
Here I am in my hospital bed
(I wish someone else was here instead)
They're all very nice – really quite sweet
And I'm certainly getting plenty to eat
But I'll never get used to the inactivity
And I'm not exactly expecting much levity
I don't go to the theatre (unfortunately not 'Barnum')
      until it's one. (o'clock that is)

Be so glad to get it all over and done
I was given QUITE an examination.
The TWO doctors were nice but I felt no elation.
200 my blood pressure reached in fine style
But it soon went down when I'd rested a while.
It was great to have you home with us
And I hope it's not hot on that d— bus.
It must be nearly time for tea
To you and Phil it's love from me.

22nd June 1982

Dear Little Lou,
so you're thirty-two!
can't quite believe it's really true –
seems but yesterday that you were born
on that cold and frosty morn.
But years have a habit of flying by –
we just can't stop them (sure like to try) –
But enough of all this backwards look –
I have shopping to do and things to cook.
I must shower and go to the shop –
poor Mr Jervis will 'blow his top'!
He likes to sit in the sun and read.
Has nothing else to do indeed.
His onions are pickled, his beer is made.
His letters are writ, his bills are paid.
Is that my fate? Heaven forbid!
But what shall I do when I lose this last 'kid'?
Shall I write a book and sew a fine seam?
And feast on strawberries, sugar and cream?
But horrors, how obese I'd get –

But right now I'll get up and take a walk
or perhaps I'll swing on the phone and talk.
Perhaps I'll sit in the sun, but whatever I do –
It's time to go!
With very much love to you and Phil
(I'm sure of this nonsense you've had your fill)
I'm glad, yesterday, you were happy
(Is it so many years since I pinned that nappy?!)
M.O.M.
(With apologies to Patience Strong*
But I bet I didn't take so long!)

Sometimes, there were letters to my children as well – like these:

Dear Josh and Zoe,
Robin and I are enclosing some money
To buy an egg (or an Easter Bunny?)
Made of chocolate, lolly and stuff
But you must stop eating when Mum says 'enough'!
Or you will be sick and come out all 'spotty'
And WE'LL get the blame
Love Robbie & Dottie.

P.S. If you would prefer,
You can buy a toy
As long as it brings you Easter joy.

---

*Patience Strong, the pen name of Winifred Emma May (1907–1990), was an English writer of sentimental poetry, song lyrics and practical psychology.

My Dear Zoe
Thank you for the little letter,
It really made me feel much better
I love the mother kangaroo
And in her pouch a baby too!
To hear from you is always nice
So write again – once or twice?
What do you want for Christmas Day
Perhaps a doll with which to play?
Or pencils, pads, a book or two?
Let me know soon – please, please do
Now it's time to say love from me
To Mummy, Josh and little Zoe
That's you!
Are you two? – no!
Snakes alive! – you're five!

Her Last Ten Years

In 1986 or '87, when all her children were finally off and away living their own lives, Mum moved into an elderly citizen's housing unit, bought for her by her sister. For the first time in her adult life, there was no need to factor rent into her weekly budget.

Mum had never had any patience with people who complained of being bored; she was always too busy – reading, cooking, sewing, going to church or fund-raising film mornings – for boredom to get a look in.

Crossword puzzles and word games had always been a regular pastime: she was an early-riser and, first thing every morning, would take a cup of coffee and a bowl of All-Bran back to bed, where she'd spend the next hour or two reading the paper, completing the daily crossword, and finding the nine-letter word hidden inside the Target Master.

Scrabble was also a favourite and the highlight of every Saturday afternoon was completing the *Advertiser* Crossquiz, usually with the help of her first-born, Rick; together, the two of them would pool their general knowledge and when that ran out, search through *Webster's Dictionary*, *Pears Encyclopaedia* or the atlas until it was done. (Crossquizzers these days probably bypass the pleasure of the hunt by going straight to Google.)

Despite such visits, as well as those of her other children and grandchildren and regular gatherings with friends for lunch or a game of Bridge, there were often times, especially in the evenings, when she felt lonely and longed for the company of 'a nice man'.

Soon after I moved back to Adelaide in 2001, into a house

just a ten-minute walk away, Mum began to show the early signs of dementia: junk mail was carefully collected and filed away with the household bills; 'intruders' moved the cassette player or left newspapers all over the floor; and the bookmark's progress through the current novel slowed for a time and then came to a complete stop.

With daily visits from carers to ensure that her medications were properly taken, and more regular visits from her children – particularly my sister, whose care of our mother over many years was unceasing and devoted – she was able to stay in her unit for several more years. However, increasing confusion and distress, especially after a short hospital stay, made it plain to us – if not to our dear mum – that she could no longer live on her own.

Mum spent the last five years of her life in a nursing home near my sister. A broken hip, and subsequent operation from which she never fully recovered, meant that she was bed-bound. Despite increasing confusion and fewer and fewer words with which to express herself, she maintained her sense of humour. Each Saturday, my sister and I visited her together; while Robin was watering the pot plants and checking Mum's clothes for washing and mending needs, and while the tea was brewing, it was my job to make Mum laugh. Usually, one of Pam Ayres's poems, or something a child in my class had said, would do it, but towards the end of her life it got harder and harder.

Her last utterance to me was a couple of weeks before her death; I was performing a mimicry of one of the 'characters' in my class and Mum, who hadn't spoken at all during our last several visits, suddenly fell into a fit of giggling and with tears in her eyes said, 'Stop being silly!'

Photo: Mum with Josh and Zoe

Christmas Day, 2001

Replete with Christmas fare, pudding put on hold,
these three most loved of people – the one who gave me life,
the two to whom I passed it – have cosseted themselves
on the couch to wait out the day, the onset of evening.

My mother is in her pink and pastel phase,
as though the fading light of her long life
demanded a gentling of clothing colour as well.

Josh is taking an all-out tilt at Cool: dark glasses, his face
arranged side-on to the camera, two fingers on his cheek,
two splayed below his mouth – the Thinker on sabbatical.

Zoe, who never moved far from 'placid baby, good sleeper',
has her head on Josh's shoulder – any place, any time good
for a nanna nap – and smiles her 'whatever' smile.

Some photographs you recognise for the earlier chapter
they represent, a place and date in a history book. Others
you see as though someone has held a mirror to your heart.

Sunday drive

Before I take my mother for a drive,
I paint the sky in the soft
pinks and blues of the baby clothes
she knitted for my children.

I fluff up the clouds,
whisk the sea till it forms
the white peaks
she likes so much,

and arrange it all at eye level
so she doesn't have to strain
past the osteoporosis
in her neck and spine.

I'm not good at conjuring
a car park near the kiosk,
so an ice cream
isn't often possible,

but the sea and sky
are always amenable.

A wooden duck, a Christmas tree ornament

        that belonged to my mother, nests among
the ink pots on my desk. It wouldn't make the cut
in a hoarder's list of 'must keep'; it's up to its red beak
in the syrup of sentiment, and all but the keenest eye
would skate over it like a fox on a frozen pond.

But as any duck in any farmyard knows
when it finds itself fox-side of the poultry pen
just as the light is dying, timing is everything.
And so it was with the little wooden duck.
And so it was with our mother.

I'll know when it's time for me to go into care, she said.
never knowing that, when the time came,
she'd be on the wrong side of knowing anything,
and that only our patience and gentle insistence
would make the time as right as ever it could be.

So too the wooden duck. On the day we moved
our mother from her home, stripped her belongings
to the short-term stay of an undertaker's anteroom,
we took a last look round and there was the duck,
its feet dug in between skirting board and carpet.

The bedside light, the pots and pans, the colander
I wish I'd kept, we dropped in the Goodwill box,
a bonanza for scavengers in the red-eyed night.
But timing is everything, and the wooden duck
won safe haven, in an ink pot nest, on my desk.

Family tree

Our mother was always one of us, part of the circle.
Aside from the odd sexual experiment
we kept nothing from her. She sobered us up,
bailed us out, dressed us down, only rarely.
But on this, her eighty-sixth birthday, our circle
has become pear-shaped. Our mother
sits at the stem, apart from its burgeoning flesh.

It's as though she's returning to the tree
to stake her claim beside her sister. Her parents
are on the sheltering bough above; she'll save a place
for her brother, tag it with her hand-bag, just in case.

If the apple doesn't fall far from the tree,
what of the pear? Thin-skinned, more easily bruised,
we can't let go. We look up at her, try to draw her back.
Gather up the photographs of holidays in Vietnam,
switch our conversation to memories of childhood –
potato printing the cubby house walls, Sunday walks
past Elephant Rock, holidays in Coffin Bay.

She leans forward as though to speak,
adjust some detail of which she was always keeper.
Smooths her stocking, checks that her hand-bag
is still beside her, sits back in her chair.
Her synapses have long been struggling
to keep pace with passing time. Now they fizzle
like a cooking pot plunged in cold water.

Light begins to seep from the sky; the air
grows cold. Our mother looks round for her stick,
takes up her bag. 'It must be time to go,' she says.
Somewhere, a pear falls; nestles into the long grass
at the foot of the tree.

General MacArthur makes a call

When my mother rang to tell me she was tired
because she'd been on a train all night returning from
a shopping trip in Melbourne, and I knew she hadn't gone
farther than the communal dining room, I told her she'd feel
better after a good night's sleep; asked if she'd had a nice time.

When she rang to ask after her children, aged eight and five,
who existed only in the movie backblock of her mind,
I assured her they were fine, hoped they wouldn't make a liar
of me by choosing that particular moment to run up and down
the hallway screaming the hollow scream of the non-existent.

When she rang a third time because an army general and all
his soldiers had arrived and expected her to put them up
for the night, I told her she was imagining things;
the war was over and there was no army, no soldiers,
no general, sitting on the couch waiting for his supper.

Didn't have the presence of mind to do my patriotic duty;
suggest she issue orders; send them all to my house.

My mother's second husband

My mother sits enveloped in a green chair.
She's puzzling over something new.
'How many times have I been married?' she asks.
'Only once, Mum,' I say.
'Or is there something you haven't told us?'

She gives me that look,
the one thing she can still find,
the look reserved for impertinent children.
'So there isn't another man then
and two young children?'

'No, Mum,' I say.
She slips back inside, pulls the lid down after her.
A minute later, emerges again.
'I'm glad,' she says.
'He wasn't a nice man. He hurt the children,
threatened to take them away from me.'

I kiss her goodbye and walk down the corridor.
Remember the children; hold out my hands,
one on either side.

By the light

I don't know what started it – the hot day perhaps,
a scorcher, my normally modest mother stripped
to bra and pants, and to take my mind off
the shocking spectacle – breasts breaking the bounds
of their double-D cups, her full-brief cottontails
stretched to their outer limits by stomach in front,
bottom behind – I sang the first song that came to mind:
By the light of the silvery moon. Badly. Deliberately off-key.

Though, when she laughed, it made her oversupply
of breast and thigh quiver like birthday jellies,
it changed my embarrassment to gratitude for this mother
and no other – not a tea-at-five, tight-lipped, tut-tutting,
neatly-trussed and tucked-away mother,
but this unrestrained, laughing, wobbling, proud-to-call-
my-own mother, this mother and no other.
So I sang it again and again, just to hear her laugh.

Fifty years later, I visit her in the nursing home.
She's locked in a cell of recessive memory;
nothing will coax her back – not photographs
of her great-grandchildren, not the one of Uncle Bob
that we know enough to keep by her bed,
not Pam Ayres's battery hen or knitting poem.
When even my best jokes fall short.
I remember *the silvery moon* and set about severing

the sound waves just as I used to.
As the last few notes skate about, slip out
from under, fall through a hole in the ice,
she turns her head to look at me and raises
her eyebrows in the gesture of mock derision
she always reserved for such silliness.
Then she stares off into the distance as though
sorting through disparate tatters of times past.

'What are you thinking, Mum?' I ask. She smiles
and says, 'I'm just wondering why we kept you.'

How to scale a fish

Holding it with your hand
and using a knife,
scrape the fish from its tail

to its head. Notice its eye,
how like your own.
Avoid holding its gaze.

Notice the scales – how perfectly shaped,
translucent, like a baby's fingernails.
Make sure you get them all.

Notice how thin is the skin of a descaled fish –
how polished to a sheen you can hold
in your hand, how easily torn.

Like your mother's skin, buried
these past five years
beneath bedridden blankets,

her knees, when the blanket fell away,
gleaming
as if unearthed in moonlight.

I call upon my father

These days, before I leave the nursing home,
I call upon my father,
dead these past thirty years,
to sit beside my mother's bed, take her hand
and repeat his vows of sixty years ago
when he was a Clark Gable lookalike
in air force uniform, cap askew,
and she wore her hair like June Allyson
in *The Glen Miller Story*.

Hope that in a few days or weeks or months
(she took her time back then
so perhaps she will again)
she'll look into the clear grey-green of his eyes
and realise the possibilities –
an eternity of encircled arms,
clouds of Palais Royal elegance,
moonlight serenading the night sky.

Then she'll smile and let him carry her
across the threshold one more time.

'She's gone…'

At three a.m. on 9 October 2011, my sister rang to say that Mum had died. I didn't need to hear the words; we could see when we visited the day before that it wouldn't be long so I knew as soon as the phone rang. My daughter, who had returned from two years living and travelling in Europe and the UK only ten days before, came into my room, hugged me and lay beside me as I tried to grow accustomed to the fact that my mother, who'd always been in the world, was no longer. How could that be? And if she wasn't in the world, where was she?

Early the next morning, my daughter and I went to the nursing home where we met my sister. For an hour or more, we sat beside Mum's bed and stared at her; could barely take our eyes from her. I remembered the poem by Henry Scott Holland that's so often read at funerals – 'I have only slipped away into the next room' – and tried to imagine her sitting in the sunroom next door, smiling to herself at the trick she had just played, moving magically through the wall into the next room.

All five of Mum's children spoke at her funeral. Each of us spoke of our own particular memories of her and there was a lot of laughter and a lot of tears. We played her favourite hymns and read her favourite Pam Ayres poem and sang, 'A, you're adorable' just as she sang it to us when we were children. One of her favourite wartime songs, 'Goodnight Sweetheart', reduced us to grief-stricken tears as all five of us walked her coffin out of the chapel and then followed the hearse down the long driveway to the road. We were pleased to witness that her final act as a presence in this world was to hold up the traffic as the hearse slid slowly out of the gate and onto the road.

Uninvited

She never entertained Death,
never sat with it over a cup of tea
or glass of wine to discuss terms:

the manner of its coming,
the price it might exact
to see her safely home.

She was always too busy
sewing, cooking, reading.
By the time it came knocking –

Death the stealthy, Death the proud –
dementia had taken all that she knew,
all that she was,

and left nothing but the poking bones
of her body and the baby bird of her mouth
opening to the touch of a teaspoon.

Last day

She was no longer able to eat or drink,
to name her world and how she would be in it
so we, her children, named it for her
and finding it wanting, unlivable, brought her
in the boat of her bed to the water's edge.
With medical say-so and Kubler-Ross
pushing us on, protecting our backs,
we told her it was time to say goodbye.
We did this. We, her children.
If only she had remained still, eyes closed, complicit.
She lifted her head and looked at us,
startled, frightened, as though we, her children,
were prising her fingers loose, pushing her
towards a place she had no wish to go.
She fell back onto the pillow
and when she closed her eyes,
the image she took with her forever imprinted
on the eggshell translucence of her eyelids,
was of her children standing around her bed
like tall wading birds that stalk the shallows
of a left-over life for a rippling of the water,
one last flash of silvered light, anything to snatch up
and keep for themselves.
We did this. We, her children.
By this means did love and betrayal
drink from the same dish.
By this means was there nothing to salvage
from our mother's last day but regret.

On the day of your death,

the lamp on the bookcase shaded its light,
the blind did its best to sidetrack the sun,
Classic FM was restricted to strings.

Your body lay posted between neat sheets.
I bent down and kissed your forehead.
Your skin was cold, paper-dry –
>   done, the labour of living;
>   done, the dark art of dying.

Your eyes were closed.
Your mouth was open in an O of surprise –
'So this is death.'

The dead are weightless, they float on a sea of air.

Was it the nurse coming in like the tide
her booming voice breaking on your shore
that forced your eyelids from their moorings?
Or did your eyes open in mute rebuke:
'Please, I'm new to this,
show some respect!'

With finger and thumb, she held your eyes shut:
you were a child well past your bedtime
wanting to stay up for the rest of the show.

I heard your indignation. Or perhaps it was mine.
I wanted her to stop. I wanted you to stay.

Echolalia

My mother gave me my name.
In the months before I was born
it rolled around in her mouth
its first calling syllable
easing into the second
ready to grace the round
and wrinkled form
in which I arrived
and will likely depart.

So when she died
my name for a time
lost its grace
became shape without shadow
question without answer,

and even now
if I were to stand on a mountain top
and shout out my name
there'd be no echo
calling back.

Her tennis trophy

How her cheeks would have flushed if she'd seen it,
resurrected and buffed for the occasion,
sitting like a communion cup on top of her coffin.

Dad was the anointed sportsman. In the first eleven at school,
only his asthma kept him from similar success
on the football oval, in the swimming pool.

A clutch of runner-up cups hid his disappointment
behind tarnished inscriptions in dark cupboard corners,
while her revered Winner Women's Doubles Belair Nov 1940

lined up, with the silver tea service, for its annual blessing,
with soft cloth and Silvo, by two young acolytes
during Boy Scouts Bobs-for-Jobs week.

And there it was again at her funeral, Dad's framed
image beside it, smiling in her reflected glory
as it shamelessly winked its celestial light.

His moustache

During a lull in proceedings – low cloud
on the mountains, or the enemy taking a day off
for the emperor's birthday – their attention turned
to facial hair, a moustache-growing competition.

At competition's end when he didn't win – despite
his handlebars, pulled straight between fingers
and thumbs, being visible when viewed from behind –
he cut off the ends, wrapped them in squares
of air force issue writing paper, labelled them
'LEFT SIDE' and 'RIGHT SIDE'
and sent them to his wife. (As you do. As he did.)

Sixty years later, when she died (he long gone),
their youngest, Stephen, hunted out the moustache ends,
preserved all these years in a box of her keepsakes,
and placed them beside her in the coffin.
It seemed the next best thing, he told the crowd
at her funeral, to cutting off a piece of her hair
and with that and the moustache ends, cloning
his parents in the back yard shed. 'And anyway,'
he said, as people smiled through their tears,
'the shed's already full of half-finished projects.'

Blue dressing gown

It takes a while to realise when your mother dies,
that the things of her lived life
are just things after all;
that her dressing table is just
a dressing table,

and that the drawer that fell
from its runners each time it was opened
and had to be lifted back into place
and jiggled and wriggled and wrestled around
and finally, frustratingly, hipped shut,

is in fact really annoying.

Some things however,
when you go to your wardrobe
and see it hanging there alongside
the can-can costume she made
for a ballet concert when you were thirteen

may take a little longer.

On becoming my mother

Today, with tea brewing in her plain brown pot
and a tarnished strainer set to catch the leaves,
I see how the early morning light cleaves
to the blue of curtains, rug, a vase. Stops
short of an even wash, becomes the haze
of gazing into mist at middle distance.
And in that pre-tea-and-toast existence
I see I've reached the penultimate phase,
a phase I've seen in the décor of another:
I am becoming my mother.
Soon I'll take to pinning my greying hair
in forties curls to grace the top of my head
then, lacking my mother's years of practised flair,
wake to the pain of a bobby-pinned bed.

In Her Own Words 2

Apart from the occasional poem (one of them included at the end of this section) Mum's writing assignments for the YWCA Creative Writing Course she completed in 1978 when she was sixty-one, are retellings of actual events, and the characters in them are family members; their names have been changed (or simply swapped around) but they are easily recognised. Perhaps she was following the advice often given to new writers – 'Write about what you know.'

Thus, in a story she titled 'The Liberated Woman', in which the first-person narrator was, like Mum, a widow who liked reading the paper and doing the crossword in bed, I became the youngest child, Jo, who at twenty-five had caused her mother some consternation by 'quite calmly' living with a man. (Unlike me, though, Jo did 'the right thing' and married the man.)

The story entitled 'Daisy', which follows, is the story of her own mother's life. Only the names have been changed: Her mother's name was Minnie; Daisy was her mother's sister.

Daisy

She was old now, almost ninety years, but her eyes were still a bright blue and her skin, though wrinkled, was soft and pink. It wasn't hard to believe that once she had been so beautiful that passers-by had turned their heads to look at her in the streets of the little English town where she lived as a girl.

Her father had always spoiled her – in fact, come to think of it, men in general spoilt her, and, of course she had always preferred them to women. No wonder really. First there had been her beloved Dad, a handsome, big man, with his blond hair and moustache, and his bright, twinkling blue eyes. He had worked as an engineer surveyor in India for many years, but although his small daughter cried for days each time he left her, she was always comforted by the thought of the letters and parcels that came to her in a steady stream until his return. Parcels of embroidered silks and muslin fit for a princess, which made her the envy of all the other girls at the small private school she attended.

Of her mother she saw little. She seemed always to be resting in bed and didn't want to be disturbed. The household management was completely taken over by Granny, a brisk, plump woman, who cooked like an angel and sewed beautifully, but was always too busy to be bothered by her granddaughter, and was glad to send her off to play with her brother David. Granny was a meticulous housekeeper, and devoted all her time and energy to caring for the house, waiting on her delicate daughter and filling the cupboards with preserves and jams. It was almost as though, having fed and clothed her grandchildren, she felt she had done her duty. Certainly she seemed to have shown no interest in their outside pursuits.

Daisy, for that was her name, and David became inseparable and together ran wild. By the time she was fourteen and should have been learning to be a lady, Daisy had become adept at all the games played by her brother and his friends. She became a familiar sight to the neighbours, riding her brother's bicycle at breakneck speed, swinging from the trees in the garden and climbing over the walls to chase balls. The pair were even known to sneak out at night to visit fairs on the common, although they knew it was strictly forbidden.

When she had turned twenty, her father decided to investigate some offers he had in Australia and wished to take Daisy with him. So without a qualm about leaving her mother and grandmother, who positively refused to make the trip, but with a heartbroken parting from David, who was to join them later, she set out for a taste of travel.

Daisy found shipboard life very much to her liking. She was never sick, even in the roughest weather, and was soon the centre of a group of young people, all intent on wringing every moment from the trip. Her father, who at this time was only forty-five, was busy with his own pleasures and left his daughter to her own devices, and the voyage, though long, passed pleasantly enough for them both.

How she loved Sydney with its sparkling harbour, busy little ferry boats, and balmy weather, and she was soon enjoying a busy round of parties and picnics. It was on one of these picnics that she met John. He was different from all the other men she had known. Oh, of course, he soon became her willing slave, but there was a quiet steadiness about his grey eyes and a shyness that appealed to her. Their love for each other developed and strengthened over the ensuing weeks and, having obtained her indulgent father's blessing, they embarked on matrimony.

What a change Daisy had to make in her way of living. She found herself quite unversed in the art of cookery, let alone household management. She had never held a needle, couldn't knit or sew, and hadn't the vaguest idea how to prepare a meal. However, she was a determined young woman and set out to learn, encouraged and helped by John, who was a patient man and not the type to expect miracles overnight. It is doubtful if the household accounts would ever have balanced were it not for the cheque that, unknown to her proud young husband, continued to arrive each week from her father.

By the time her first child was born, a boy, who was her pride and joy, Daisy had mastered the culinary arts, learnt to care for her house and even managed to knit small garments for her son with creditable neatness. Later, two girls joined the family, who she also loved dearly, but her firstborn always had a special place. Even now, so many years later, although always pleased to see her daughters, it is the visits from her son that are the highlights of her dull days.

Yes, the opposite sex had always attracted her. It is still the men in her past life who constantly people her waking thoughts and dreams. The handsome generous father, her beloved brother, companion in so many childhood adventures and pranks, who had died tragically in the first world war, and, of course, her devoted husband, her lover and her strength with whom she had shared sixty wonderful years and, of course, her son, her eldest child who still brought her flowers, remembered the sweets she preferred and held her hand while he told her the things she wanted to hear.

Yes, she was old now and since coming to 'this place', going over her past life was her chief occupation – so much more pleasant than living in the present where each day merged into the next, so exactly alike were they. Life had become just one long round of being bathed, dressed, fed and visited by 'her girls'. (Of course, they, too, were growing old now but to her they were still girls.) Then it was bedtime and she was left to her dreams, dreams that were of England and peopled by the friends of her past and especially the men she loved. Sometimes she found it difficult to know which was the reality and which the dream.

Of course, there were nights when the dreams became frightening and she woke to the sound of her own voice calling out. Always the same name was on her lips. Funny, that. Why wasn't she calling out for her indulgent father or her dear kind beloved husband who had been such a delightful friend and companion? Why was the name that was always on her lips 'Mother'?

Mum's notebooks

Mum started several notebooks – I bought her so many, after all – and didn't fill any of them. Apart from the start she made on her life story, she used them for all sorts of things: words she came across and wanted to remember (plethora, milieu, asthetic), the instructions for knitting lace, a pattern for a teddy bear, favourite hymns ('The day thou gavest Lord is ending, Morning has broken'), a list of the seven deadly sins…

In one, she had copied some quotable quotes from her daily reading of the *Advertiser* newspaper; amongst them, these:

> You'll always stay young if you live honestly, eat slowly, sleep sufficiently, work industriously, worship faithfully – and lie about your age.

> A man works all his life to keep the wolf from the door, and then his daughter grows up and brings him home.

> Too much of a good thing is wonderful. (Mae West)

Also included in her jottings was W.H. Auden's poem 'Funeral Blues', and in the same notebook, signed DEA, the poem that follows…

Morning

It was early when I arose
Dewdrops glistened on one perfect rose
I made a vow – I meant it then –
No longer would I lie till ten,
But be up at dawn when the world is quiet –
The world looks fresher by early light
>   It was early when I arose.

It was late when I said 'goodnight'
Such a busy day – no time to write –
Just chores to do and folk to see
A rush to the shops for something for tea
Then there was washing and ironing too
So little time so much to do
>   It was late when I said 'goodnight'

It was late when I left my bed
The sky was gloomy and grey overhead
The endless day held nothing of cheer
I dragged through the chores with thoughts so drear
And vowed that tomorrow I'd lie till noon
And even then would be too soon
>   To rise and face this life again…

Ah! The sun shines again, there's no more rain

Oh what a beautiful day!

Afterword

I began working on this book in early 2013, a year or so after Mum's death, then set it aside several times while other things in my life took precedence: teaching contracts, annual visits to my son and his wife in London, the completion and publication of a collection of my poems.

Now here it is five years on, my teaching career all but done, both of my children and their partners and a child apiece living nearby, the sun well over the yardarm of my days – and where was I when that happened I should like to know? – and it's finally finished…

Or as finished as it ever will be, given that I still write about her sometimes…

Meet my mother

After Karin Gottshall

Sometimes I say I'm going to meet my mother just because
I like saying it. I like it for its mouth feel and pleasure:
…meet my mother.

It was a phone call at three a.m. drove those words away.
Five years later, with no conscious effort on my part,
they followed an overgrown but still navigable path

all the way to my mouth that they might line up
and spill from it just as they used to:
I'm going to meet my mother.

Some days, I go to the Broadway Café and sit at a table
for two, one with a view of the sea. She loved the sea.
Mothers come and go, some with daughters, some not.

Each time the door opens, I look up and imagine her
standing there in the Chanel suit she made herself;
a smile crinkling her eyes, her hair blown about a bit.

Then, the sea suitably gazed upon in her stead,
I check my phone and pretend to read a message
that could well be from her in which she says,

'Sorry, the cake's taking an age to cook,
can't think why, what about tomorrow?'

Mum's Recipes

Burnt Butter Biscuits

¼ lb butter
½ lb sugar
1 egg
50z S R Flour
½ teaspoon vanilla

Put butter in pan &
heat until brown — cool
a little — pour into it
sugar & beaten egg. Add
S R Flour & vanilla. Put
balls of mixture on cool
slide & half an almond
each. Bake in moderate
oven about ¼ hour.

Glug

2 cups rolled oats
1 cup sugar
1 cup coconut
1 cup SR flour
1 egg
1 small tsp carb soda
250g butter
2 tbsp golden syrup

Melt butter with golden syrup. Let cool.
Beat egg with carb soda.
Mix in egg.
Add dry ingredients and mix well.
Press into greased lamington tray.
Bake at 375°F until brown (20–30 mins).

Joy's Jubilee Cake

1 cup sugar
2 cups mixed fruit
1 cup water
50g butter
1 egg
2 cups SR flour

Put sugar, fruit, water and butter into saucepan.
Bring to boil.
When cool, add egg and flour.
Place in two log tins.
Bake for 40–45 mins in a moderate oven.
When cool, ice with plain white icing.

Burnt-butter Biscuits

125g butter
250g sugar
1 egg
150g SR flour
½ tsp vanilla
shelled and halved almonds

Heat butter in saucepan until brown. Cool.
Mix in sugar and beaten egg.
Add SR flour and vanilla and mix.
Place balls of the mixture onto oven tray.
Put half almond on each.
Bake in moderate oven 10–15 mins.

Cheese Rusks

1½ cups SR flour
1 cup grated cheese
2 tbsp butter
2 tbsp milk
1 tsp salt
½ tsp mustard
2 eggs
¼ tsp cayenne pepper

Rub butter into flour, salt and cayenne pepper.
Add grated cheese.
Mix in beaten eggs, milk and mustard.
Knead into a ball and roll out to 2cm thickness.
Cut into fingers.
Place on greased oven tray.
Bake in hot oven (220°F) 10–15 mins.
Take from oven and slice in half lengthways.
Place on low shelf in low oven (100°F) until really dry.

List of Photographs

Cover image	Mum, aged twenty-four
page 9	Mum in her mid-thirties
page 13	Childhood photo: (left to right) Mum, Dick, Joy
page 29	Mum and Dad on their wedding day, 24 December 1941
page 47	Mum on the SS *Arcadia*, 1977
page 59	Aerogramme from Mum to me
page 83	Mum and my sister Robin, 1992
page 99	Mum with her children, 1997: (back, left to right) Rick, me, Mum, Stephen; (in front) Robin, John
page 111	Mum's mother, Minnie Marshall (née Davies), aged eighteen, 1907

Note

This book is a personal memoir of my mother and my relationship with her. Undoubtedly, my sister and brothers have different memories – both of her, and of some of the events described.

www.ingramcontent.com/pod-product-compliance
Lightning Source LLC
Chambersburg PA
CBHW070915080526
44589CB00013B/1303